HOW THE BANK SCREWS YOU

Henry H. Petersohn

Table of Contents

1. BEFORE WE HAD BANKS...2

2. WHY GOLD AND SILVER...4

3. KEEP MONEY IN VAULTS AND CHANGE OWNERSHIP VIA THE PHONE 5

4. LET'S USE PAPER INSTEAD OF COINS 6

5. WHERE'S YOUR MONEY TODAY - MOVING MONEY IN YOUR ACCOUNT 8

6. How Banks Might Disadvantage You with Credit Card Practices. Stay Informed to Avoid Financial Pitfalls. 11

Your friendly bank is a helpful institution. They love being helpful since they are making money servicing your accounts. Your money is used to pay everyone's salary and build comfortable offices. They are happy to present all types of offers to manage your finances including checking accounts, savings accounts, CDs, Money market opportunities, mortgage loans, personal loans, credit cards, and investment opportunities. Wonderful! But remember they are doing it to be able to charge you for all their services whether you use them or not.

How they operate can be a hazard to your personal finances so get a better deal by understanding why banking was invented and what is going on behind the scenes.

1. BEFORE WE HAD BANKS

If you grew grapes, how many pounds would you trade for a loaf of bread or a chicken? How much corn would you trade for a goat or some grapes? The people you would trade with often lived at a distance and just getting back and forth with your products took time over unpaved roads and paths. This was a problem since you only had so many hours in the day to raise animals and crops and make grapes into wine. You and your family had to work from dawn to dusk to survive.

One early way to trade without having to carry chickens, driving goats. or carrying heavy bundles was to use bricks of tea or bags of salt as money. There was a practical problem for most people. How could they determine the quality of the product they were using so they would know how much it was worth as money.

This problem created a need for trading middle-men who specialized in evaluating the quality of the product and could offer a reasonable price. The scarcity and later appearance of gemstones, silver, and gold made them attractive to the eye and their small weight quickly brought them into use as a type of money.

2. WHY GOLD AND SILVER

4

Gold and silver coins were much preferred as money since they take little space and would not be bothered by cold or reasonable heat or water. In actual use, however, some people would attempt to steal a little of the metal by shaving the edges. To prevent this, such coins were produced with grooved (milled) edges.

3. KEEP MONEY IN VAULTS AND CHANGE OWNERSHIP VIA THE PHONE

Moving gold and silver was a serious problem so armored trucks and guards are needed. Of course, it is much easier physically, if the gold and silver could be just left in a protected vault and the ownership transferred by a simple phone call. However, such an easy authorization process could be interrupted by adroit telecommutions hackers, so special processes are followed by the banks, the Federal Reserve system and the Comptroller of the Currency to stop this tactic.

4. LET'S USE PAPER INSTEAD OF COINS

Even with gold, silver, and later copper and nickel coins, there was not enough currency available for the public to use for everyday buying and selling. Physical minting and then handling and storage of coins was costly.

Using paper has it's problems. The general public has to believe that the paper money is as valuable as coins, easier to use and can be obtained at any bank. However, the paper has to be printed. It also has to be replaced when it wears out. Paper can be counterfeited and, in some places, loses its value, largely since the government that issues the paper is not trusted. This has essentially happened to countries like Germany, Italy and Argentina although it was often not aways obvious. In contrast, the US Government has never had a policy of devaluing currency. It also has a policy of tracking down down counterfeiters and quickly collects and destroys counterfeit bills. It does a stellar job of keeping money flowing safely

Almost every country prints and uses its own paper money. In the US we talk dollars, in England we talk pounds, in France we had francs and now Euros, in Italy we had lira and now Euros.

5. WHERE'S YOUR MONEY TODAY - MOVING MONEY IN YOUR ACCOUNT

Many Federal and State agencies have established rules and processes for all banks to insure that money moves safely. When the Federal government spends money to individuals, i.e. tax refunds, social security checks, and pension payments, they generally send a single payment to a bank along with a list of the payees. Banks respond by crediting each separate account in that list within a day. Federal grant money is commonly sent electronically to a grantee's account in time to allow the grantee to issue paychecks to their employees on the same or the next day.

Banks and financial Institutions take their time moving your money. They don't want any error on their part. They may hold up issuing a check or honoring a credit card charge or the hint of an error because they are paranoid about the possibility of fraud and the possible loss of many accounts if this occurred. As a result,you will be called and your response carefully analyzed before they will move your money. The effect is that your payment may not arrive at its destination for ten days - maybe longer - once they actually put it in the mail - electronic or postal. Since the payment is out of their hands once sent, they leave it to you to find out if the payment was actually received at the destination and completed. If your payee is concerned because the money is not in their hands, the bank tells them you should have sent the payment sooner. You get blamed.

If you are transferring money between your accounts at the same bank, i.e. paying a credit card account at the bank with money from your checking account at the same bank, you can often find this payment is completed in a few minutes. If you move money from an investment account at your bank to your checking account at the same bank, this may take 3 to 5 business days and sometimes more. They don't do processing on Friday after closing time, on Saturday, and not on a Sunday or holiday. Since you now know that the bank may delay making a payment, it is a smart thing to pay all bills at least 7 – 10 days early. Beware, if your payments are delayed because your bank was slow in processing, that information goes against your credit records, not against the bank. This type of misleading information can also cause a job application to be tossed aside or a job promotion go to another person because it was late. The bank claims it is innocent. This is your problem. It does not intend to screw you but you become an innocent victim with no recourse.

6. 6 How Banks Might Disadvantage You with Credit Card Practices. Stay Informed to Avoid Financial Pitfalls.

While credit cards can be convenient and offer benefits like rewards and points, some bank practices can lead to financial pitfalls for consumers. Here are several ways banks might disadvantage you with their credit card facilities:

1) **High-Interest Rates**: Many credit cards come with high-interest rates, especially if you carry a balance from month to month. This can quickly lead to substantial debt if you're not careful.

2) **Hidden Fees**: Credit cards often come with a variety of fees, including annual fees, late payment fees, balance transfer fees, and foreign transaction fees. These can add up and increase your overall cost of using the card.

3) **Complex Terms and Conditions**: The terms and conditions of credit cards are often lengthy and written in complex legal language, making it difficult for consumers to fully understand the potential pitfalls.

4) **Minimum Payment Trap**: Banks often allow you to make a small minimum payment on your credit card balance each month. While this might seem manageable, it can lead to a cycle of debt, as paying only the minimum means you'll be paying interest on the remaining balance.

5) **Introductory Offers**: Banks frequently use attractive introductory offers, such as low or zero interest rates for an initial period, to entice new customers. However, once the introductory period ends, the interest rates can spike dramatically.

6) **Changing Terms**: Banks reserve the right to change the terms of your credit card agreement, including interest rates and fees. This can happen with little notice and can catch consumers off guard.

7) **Credit Limit Increases**: Banks might automatically increase your credit limit, encouraging you to spend more. While this might seem like a benefit, it can lead to higher debt and increased interest payments.

8) **Rewards Programs**: While rewards programs can offer benefits, they often encourage higher spending. Additionally, the value of rewards can be less than the cost of interest and fees if balances are not paid in full each month.

9)	**Payment Processing Times**: Some banks process payments in ways that maximize interest charges. For example, they might take longer to process your payment, resulting in additional interest charges.

10)	**Deferred Interest Promotions**: Some credit cards offer deferred interest promotions on purchases, which means interest is only charged if the balance is not paid off by a certain date. However, if you miss that date, you could be charged interest retroactively from the date of purchase.

Understanding these practices can help you make more informed decisions about using credit cards and managing your finances. Always read the fine print and consider the long-term implications of your credit card usage.

About the Author

Henry H. Petersohn

A Ph.D is a research and teaching degree. Petersohn previously taught business management and statistics and has written on computer topics. He personally had to undergo serious cardiac surgery and a stressful recovery and that involved Johns Hopkins and the Med-Star Hospital in DC. He also had to deal with more than two dozen family medical issues that pushed him into working with London's National Health System and Venice's Mesre as well as the Cleveland Clinic in Cleveland and St. Joseph's in Phoenix. He was drawn into extensive medical research as family issues became serious which spurred a deep interest in researching medical journals and reports from sources such as NIH, Johns Hopkins, UCLA, Emory University, and the MAYO Clinic.

Dedication

"I have to dedicate this book not only to my beautiful little Liberty, who is greatly loved, but also to her beautiful Mom and my dear friend, who is greatly loved as well. Additionally, to the rest of my family, the ones who never gave up on a lost boy like me. I love you all to the Moon and back."

Contents

Dedication

Chapter 1: Adventurous Life in Kentucky 5

Chapter 2: The Mysterious Cave at Devil's Backbone 7

Chapter 3: The Secret of the Mysterious Cave 10

Chapter 4: The Vanishing Fairies and Mysterious Cave................................ 13

Chapter 5: The Cave of Nightmares and Surprises.. 17

Chapter 6: A Plan in the Making... 20

Chapter 7: Operation Fairy SWAT & Uncle Delbert's Wisdom..................... 23

Chapter 8: The Fairy Capture Plan 30

Chapter 9: The Ogre's Defeat and a New World... 34

Chapter 10: The Mysterious Stones and Vanishing Cave 40

Chapter 1
Adventurous Life in Kentucky

In eastern Kentucky, there was a simple and religious family. Mom was Mrs. Trisha, and Dad was Mr. Jerry Senior. They had three kids: Jerry, who was twelve, Kevin, who was ten, and the youngest, Liberty, who was two months old.

Back in those days, life was not easy. They didn't have modern stuff like washing machines or self-rinsing cycles. Even the toilets were not located within the house; instead, they had to make their way to small structures known as outhouses.

Dad, Mr. Jerry Senior, had to go to work every day to make money for the family. Lots of people in Kentucky were doing the same thing to survive, and even today, not much has changed.

In the mountains where they lived, work often took many days or even weeks. Jerry and Kevin, the two brothers, had to take care of the gardens, animals, and everything else that needed doing. But they didn't mind doing their part.

After they finished their work each day, the boys went on exciting adventures. They explored the mountains, went into caves and old mines, swung on vines, and caught crawdads. They loved anything that made their hearts race and made them feel like adventurers.

Chapter 2

The Mysterious Cave at Devil's Backbone

The mountains looked like a city, each one having a name. One of them played a crucial role in our story, known as the "Devil's Backbone."

"Now, let's continue the story, but remember a few things, okay? Shh, shh, shh."

After a tiring day of carrying water and working in the gardens, the boys waited in the yard for their mom's approval. It was the same routine they knew by heart. "Don't wander too far. Stay close enough to hear me when I call, and if you see strangers, get back here. Got it?" Their mom reminded them.

"Yes, Mom," the boys replied, taking her words to heart, but they were off like a shot, eager to explore the woods.

Sometimes their cousins joined them, and they could go further because they knew their mom would be busy with her sisters, not paying much attention to their whereabouts.

Jerry, the oldest, had a wild side, and two young boys left on their own could be as wild as bucks.

These boys knew the land perfectly, but they rarely ventured near the Devil's Backbone. However, on a warm summer day, they decided to investigate.

To reach it, they knew they had gone about half a mile beyond their usual limits, just in case their mom decided to look for them instead of shouting for them.

Now, back to the story. They slid down banks, crossed the creek bed, passed the old giant maple, and climbed the high bank before they reached the Devil's Backbone. Normally, there was a broad swing using grapevines to get there, but today, they were puzzled and shocked.

"Kevin, do you see what I see?" Jerry asked Kevin.

"Hmm, I don't remember a cave being there," Kevin replied, both boys scratching their heads.

"A cave, Kevin! Where did it come from?" Jerry said sarcastically, walking around this new giant structure that had suddenly appeared in their playground.

"Now I know," Jerry stated. "We usually swing right through here." He pointed to where they had come from. "And then we would..." Jerry stopped mid-sentence, his eyes widening.

Staring above Kevin, then below him, he now hurries behind his big brother with the thought that a snake, bear, or something life-threatening had come from the cave behind him. But to his soon-to-be dreadful surprise, it was neither. They would soon realize it was much worse.

"Hello, little ones," a small, dark, mischievous voice says, emerging from the shadow of the cave again.

"Hello, little one," Jerry replies, reaching behind his self to make sure his little brother is standing so he doesn't trip. "Who are you, and where did you come from, Miss Fairy, is it?" Jerry asks with a stern voice, thinking in the back of his mind, "I am the bigger brother, and this fairy is or might as well be on our land."

"It's okay, Jerry, is it?" The voice continues. "And your little brother behind you—what is your name, little one?" "My name is..." Shh, "Kevin, don't tell her your name," Jerry interrupts quickly. "We aren't supposed to talk to strangers, flying or not. How did you know my name anyway?"

"Too cute, little ones," the fairy starts getting closer to the boys, her eyes narrowing as if she could see through the boys, and the boys do the same. Then she repeats, "Too cute, little ones," with dark blue eyes and her silver dress shimmering as she flies to and from the boys.

Chapter 3

The Secret of the Mysterious Cave

"Boys, time to come home," they hear faintly in the distance. "Go inside, look, go look," the fairy insists, trying to drown out the sound of their MOM, who had now given the boys the dreaded (1). With this, the boys shake their heads as if they were in a trance or something.

"Sorry, shiny pants," Jerry tells her, pushing his little brother first and putting his brother before himself. "See you later," Jerry turns back to say, and about that time, they hear (2). So they pick up the pace through the creek and back up and over the other side. Then down the last stretch. They see the tree line, and before the dreaded (3) can leave their mom's lips, she sees her two white-haired, blue-eyed boys break through the bushes.

"Okay, Mom, we're here," Kevin yells. "MOM, you know it would be much easier if you counted to ten. We almost got killed trying to get here."

"Yeah, but three is funnier," MOM says with a laugh.

"Reality, Mom," Jerry says with half a grin. But truth be told, a lot of the time, if they hadn't made it back, they'd get a 2 1/2 or even a 2 3/4, so it's really like a good five. But, out of respect for their mom and not to upset her, they go as she says.

"To get home with no trouble, it's been a good day," Jerry thinks to himself as they go down the hall to their room, which was three in one that their dad built for the boys from his garage years ago. But truth be told, for its time, it was nice.

One side of the room was nice and neat, with clothes folded and everything in an orderly manner. The other side, however, looked like a disaster area that even FEMA or the Red Cross couldn't begin to save.

"I mean, really, Kevin. If you can't put your dirty clothes in their place, don't ask me for clean ones," Jerry stated, scolding Kevin as he saw him with his shoes in hand. He just stated the obvious.

"Come on, Bubby, it's just a pair of socks. Mine are still wet on the line," Jerry added sarcastically. "Kevin, you only call me 'Bubby' when you want or need something." To avoid trouble and thinking of their mom, he tossed Kevin a pair he had already laid out for him.

"But really, can you believe what we saw?" Kevin asked, sitting beside his brother, not sure what to think or say. "I know, and she really wanted us to go into that cave for some reason."

"I thought I was going to have to knock her out if she got any closer."

"Yeah, I was going to bite her, scratch her, or something," Kevin said, jumping up from the bed and swinging in the air. "Okay, okay, Rocky, calm down. But really, Kevin, let's not mention this to anyone," Jerry said with a nervous voice.

"A freaking fairy?" Kevin repeated, shaking his head as he walked over to his bed.

"But seriously, promise me you won't say anything," Jerry asked Kevin.

"Huh, about what? That we almost got eaten by a fairy in the woods by a cave that appeared out of nowhere?" He said this to his brother with a grin. They both laughed when they heard it out loud. "Sounds crazy, huh?" Jerry said as they climbed into bed.

"Here, boys, kiss your sister good night," Mom said, swinging the door open and walking over to Jerry first. She held their little sister out for him to hug and kiss. Before Jerry lay back down, he leaned back up and kissed his mom on the cheek, then moved over to Kevin.

"Oh, before I go, boys, your dad called to tell you he loved you as well, and he'll be home in a few weeks."

"Yes!" the boys replied to their mom, both lying down with smiles across their faces.

Chapter 4

The Vanishing Fairies and Mysterious Cave

The next day, the boys rushed through their chores, tending to the gardens and carrying water for washing and rinsing clothes, as well as anything else they knew their mom needed to be done before her inspections.

"Okay, Mom, we're done," Jerry hollered in the house. After inspecting everything, she looked at the boys, as if she were going to point out something they had missed. But her expression changed from a serious look to a warm smile, and she said, "Go on, have fun. Just stay close so we can hear you," they say before she can, and the boys sprint into the woods.

Back through the winding trail, up and over the banks, through the creek, and back to Devil's Backbone. Peeking over the bank, both boys hesitated before revealing themselves, in case the fairy was there. They both agreed that something felt off about everything.

Now, with the cave in sight, to their surprise, they saw two more fairies in front of the cave, sitting on a small stone as if waiting for something or someone. Overwhelmed by curiosity, the boys climbed over the top and approached the cave. Before they could ask the new fairies anything, a silver-dressed fairy emerged from the cave's dark shadow, grinning.

She began to introduce the two new fairies, who remained silent with scared looks on their faces. First, they looked at the silver-dressed fairy, then at the boys. Jerry caught on, sending chills up his spine, but he and Kevin said nothing; they nodded and smiled. It was then that the silver fairy gave the other two a nod. Like in a trance, the two got up and walked past the boys without a word, vanishing into the cave.

"Hey, where did they go, Shiny?" Kevin couldn't help but ask, now certain that something strange was happening.

To Kevin's surprise, the silver fairy landed in front of him, staring with her deep blue, sinister eyes. She replied to Kevin, "You want to go in, little ones?" pointing to the cave.

"Not right now, Shiny," Jerry intervened, putting his arm around his little brother and pulling him away from her and the cave. But a gust of wind came, and she flew above the boys, pointing at the cave. "What harm do you think would happen? Why don't you want to see it? Go on, little ones, for a while; there are many other little ones inside." She drew closer, circling the boys, repeating, "Go, little ones, go and see."

In the nick of time, they heard their mom shout (1) with a look of anger.

Without hesitation, the boys took off, running back toward home, shouting, "Talk later, sorry, we got to go," not looking back.

As they emerged from the tree line, they noticed their mom was not on the porch. "Huh, where is Mom? I know I heard her," Jerry said, entering the back door. "Yeah, me too," Kevin agreed.

Then, they heard their mom in the living room with the TV blaring, "Hey, boys, hurry, look. Do you know these kids? They disappeared a few days ago, close to here. They're not sure if they were kidnapped or what. They could have run off, as far as they know."

"Not sure, Mom," Jerry told her. "No, I do either," Kevin said as well.

"Well, like I always say," she reminded them as she picked up Baby Liberty from her crib.

"Yeah, Mom, we remember," Kevin said, following his older brother down the hall to their bedroom.

As soon as the door shut, Jerry began pacing the floor, a scared look on his face. "Kevin, the fairies... but could they have something to do with those kids?"

"Huh, what do you mean?" Kevin asked.

"It's strange, the way they kept staring at us with that scared look on their faces, as if they needed help or something."

"I know, but..." Kevin replied, sitting beside Jerry on his bed because he was afraid to walk over to his bed, which was a mess. "Kevin, go clean your side and make your bed, for Pete's sake," Kevin grumbled but complied.

"Well, should we stay away from there, then, Bubby, or do you think it's not that big of a deal?" Kevin asked his big brother.

"Hold on, do you think we should let them scare us off our own land, Kevin? Would Dad have let them scare him off our land, Bub?"Jerry asked Kevin, who was now helping him fix his bed and clean his room,

"Well, what do you think?"

"I'm thinking inside the cave will tell us everything we need to know, but I'm also thinking that everything we don't want to know is happening after we leave."

Before we got back, Jerry explained to Kevin, "So, what's your plan, buddy?" Kevin asked in a shaky voice, afraid to even inquire. He couldn't shake the image of those evil blue eyes of the silver-dressed fairy and the unsettling vibe she gave off.

The boys began devising a plan, but they first finished cleaning up Kevin's horrific side of their room. First, the boys created an official work area they named the "war zone." This signified their commitment. They worked to avoid waking their sister. The first step was covering the windows, and then they set out to create a foolproof plan to discover what's going on with the silver-pants figure and the mysterious cave, even uncovering what happened to the missing children.

One thing was certain: neither Jerry nor Kevin would let fear stand in their way. Jerry was a big fan of war novels and had paid close attention to his uncle's war stories shared during their hunting trips.

"Wait, you want to go into the cave?" Kevin asked, surprised. "Inside it? Us, in the cave?" He inquired as Jerry finished a few things on the floor, scratching his head while jotting down notes.

"Yes, Kevin, but we'll need to sneak out. Let's get some sleep now," Jerry suggested, turning off the lights.

"Good night, buddy," Kevin replied. Off to sleep they went.

Chapter 5

The Cave of Nightmares and Surprises

That night, unlike any other night, both boys had nightmares of fairies chasing them and a giant ogre with a chain around the boys, pulling them into the cave. Then, at the same time, both boys woke from their sleep, looking around their room and then at each other. At the same time, they said, 'In the cave.'

The next morning, as early as they awoke, the boys headed out. 'So, we got to go into the cave, really, bub?' Kevin asked Jerry again, opening the back door as quietly as possible. 'Hopefully, Mom won't wake up,' Jerry whispered, pushing the door shut. Through the yard and into the woods, the boys traveled, being as quiet as possible this time, not to give away their whereabouts. 'Man, I had some crazy dreams last night,' Jerry told his brother. 'Yeah, me too, and I kept seeing this...' And before he could say it, Jerry stopped and looked back, saying, 'An ogre.' 'Yes,' Kevin told him as he followed his brother up the bank of the backbone, peeking over again. Both boys remained quiet. 'How is this possible?' But in the back of their heads was the thought of the kids that could be vanishing next, or even their mom.

To the boys' surprise, they weren't staring at a fairy anymore. The boys turned and slid back to be sure they couldn't be seen.

'That's not what it is, bub. That's not an old lady from my dream.' 'Yeah, nor mine,' Jerry told his little brother, putting their pocket knives away as if they were carrying swords. 'Well, that's not what I expected.' 'What the heck?' Kevin let out a little more than he expected. 'Shhh,' Jerry whispered, looking again but not believing it. 'Now, that ain't no fairy, is all I know,' Jerry told his brother. 'Well, what is she?'

'I am not sure, but I've got a book that might have our answer.' So, the boys lay there watching this lady with what seemed to be a bright light all around her, talking to the new little fairies, and they would talk back. Yet, the boys were too far away to hear anything, and they couldn't see her face or theirs. They were sitting on stones, facing the opposite direction, in front of the cave. Then, to the boys' surprise, a loud, guttural roar came from inside the cave. The boys gasped as they felt a tremor in the ground. The boys' hearts dropped as this creature, looking like a real-life Shrek, emerged from the shadow of the cave. Bent over, the boys' eyes widened, and they froze with fear, watching this giant creature grab the light lady by her neck, pulling her back into the cave but leaving the little fairies. As soon as they were out of sight, a great flash of blue light emanated from inside the cave.

Then, to the boys' surprise, out came Ole Silver Pants, but she looked so different, like a much eviler version of herself, with bigger teeth and dark red eyes. Even her silver dress seemed to be a darker silver, or at least it seemed that way to the boys, who were staring now, not knowing what to do. Then, to their surprise, she started shouting in an evil-sounding language to the little fairies, and within a second, they all rushed back into the cave with a blue flash, the fairies, and the cave.

Were gone "What the heck?" Jerry shouts, jumping up and over and sliding down to where the cave once was.

"Bub, wait!" Kevin shouts back at his brother, not sure what to think about everything he just saw.

"Kevin, come here!" Jerry shouts to his little brother. "Yes, I flipping did," Kevin says, now climbing up and over the bank cautiously, not knowing what to think. "Can you believe this, really?" Kevin continues, grabbing his brother by the shoulders. Both boys look around, and then both boys notice the footprints from the fairies, but not just the fairies, also the giant footprints of the ogre as well.

"Okay, Kevin, we got to go now," Jerry says.

"Huh, why?" Kevin asks. "The way that everything disappeared, don't you think they could just reappear?" Kevin is afraid.

So, back through the woods, up and over the bank.

"Hold on, Kevin, should we go back?"

"Normally, we wouldn't have been there until after a while, right?" Jerry explains.

"Yeah, normally, but we really didn't do our chores or anything yet," Kevin reminds his big brother. "After everything we've seen, we're going to need a much better plan." Then, as the words leave his mouth, the boys hear their mom, who is not far from where they are.

Chapter 6
A Plan in the Making

"Here, Mom, we're here," Jerry shouts to his mom, hurrying through the tree line so she can see the boys.

"Where have you boys been?" their mom asks, rocking their little sister on the porch.

"We went ginseng hunting, Mom, and hunting for bloodroot." Kevin is quick to answer his mom, showing her some weeds he had grabbed a moment ago. Hoping his brother didn't look closer.

"Okay, get your butt in there and get your chores done, then you can go root hunting, alright?"

"Yes, Mother," the boys assure their mom and start doing their chores.

While in the middle of filling their buckets for washing clothes, Kevin asks his brother sincerely. "Bub, would you come looking for me if I disappeared?" Kevin says this with a half-grin on his face.

"Really, Kevin, why would you even ask?" Jerry says, looking at his brother like he's crazy.

"Listen, who would I be without you having my back, really? Little brother, I'd have a lot more work to do than we already have," Jerry says with a laugh, joking with his little brother, trying to ease his mind.

Then, to the boys' surprise, their mom comes out and calls the boys in. Through the front door, Jerry and Kevin followed.

"Hey, boys, I've got to run to your aunt's. Liberty has a fever, so I'm going to get her some medicine."

"Yeah, sure, Mom, we'll be fine."

The boys assure their mom, never wanting her to worry. After finishing their chores and seeing their mom off, the boys rush into the house, locking the door behind them.

"Okay, Kevin, to the war zone," Jerry tells Kevin with narrowed eyes and a half smile on his face. Then both boys head down the hall to their bedrooms.

"Bub, what the heck is going on around here?" Jerry asks Kevin, closing the bedroom door behind him. "I know. Can you believe everything, really?" Kevin replies back, sitting on a pile of clothes beside his bed that he was supposed to have brought out to Mom earlier.

Now, just patiently waiting for Jerry to devise a greater plan. Their situation went from bad to severe after finding out there were even more mythical creatures to deal with.

"Well, bub," Jerry asks Kevin after a few moments of contemplating, "you want the good news or the bad news?"

"Just say it, bub," Kevin is quick to ask.

"Well, really, I have no idea," Jerry says with a worried look on his face, and Kevin notices it.

"I say we should go talk to Uncle Delbert," Kevin says, "yeah, good idea, and act like we're playing or something just to see what he tells us."

"Yeah, exactly," Kevin agrees with his brother. "Dang, little brother, you're too smart." Jerry is quick to applaud his brother's idea.

But first, let's set up some alarms around here in case they do come back and come looking for us down here. Kevin agrees, pushing clothes under his bed off to the tree line with spools of fishing line and a bag of cans, as well as a pack of fireworks that you pull apart to make explode.

Chapter 7

Operation Fairy SWAT & Uncle Delbert's Wisdom

After a few hours of tying lines and setting up a defense line around the yard so they're not caught off-guard, the boys head over to Uncle Delbert's, which was at the mouth of their holler. Bartley Hollow was the name, and they lived at the main end.

After a few knocks, they hear a shotgun go off out back, so the boys run around, wondering what was happening. Uncle Delbert hollers not to get shot by mistake coming around the house.

"Yeah, hey boys, what brings you here?" He asks his little nephews, hugging them both at the same time in his big, oversized arms.

"Well," Jerry starts off, sitting beside his uncle on his big green swing, "we have been playing a game and wanted to know what you thought."

"Okay, ask me. If we were attacked by killer fairies or ogres, what would you do to protect yourself?"

"Well, flying fairies?" he asks Jerry. "Yeah," Kevin speaks up, "flying and big giant ogres."

"Well, for one, I'd get my rifle out." "Well," Jerry stops him, "what if you were us with no rifle?"

"Oh, I understand, boys. Well, I'd get me a bunch of sticks, big one's, even because I know you boys are strong. You remember all the different traps I taught you boys to make?" He asks the boys, staring with a serious look on his face. "Just make them bigger. Then, instead of the small holes we dug for the rabbits and squirrels, just dig them much bigger." He explains, "Now you're staying with me."

"Yes, Uncle Delbert," the boys assure him, taking in every word.

"Now, you know the string we would tie off the traps with?" The boys nod with serious looks on their faces.

"Okay, I got you." Jerry jumps up, grabbing Kevin by the arm. Quickly giving Uncle Delbert a hug, they head back home. "Okay, boys, tell your mom and dad I said hi!" Uncle Delbert shouts and waves as the boys run out of sight.

"Kevin, where is the rope we had and all that tennis net Dad brought home a few months ago?" Jerry asks his brother as they head back up the hill, contemplating a foolproof plan for the second time. But this time, Jerry was going to defend his house or die trying.

After arriving back at the house, the boys start to devise their plan, first gathering all their material and moving it behind the tree line in case their mom shows up. Shovels, mattocks, and everything else they figured they may need, covering it with leaves, getting all prepared before they head in for the night. All this running and prepping had worn the boys out, but before they had gone to sleep, they took one last journey to go look and see if the cave was still there or if they really still had anything to worry about.

Then, peeking over the bank as usual, to their surprise, there she was, the light lady, with what looked like a giant chain around her neck, sitting and talking to what were now three fairies, little ones. So, upon seeing this, the boys weren't taking any chances and resisted going back to the cave. They slid back down without a word and got back home as fast as possible. Straight to their bedroom after locking the back door, and after cleaning up, they were off to bed.

"Bub," Kevin asks quietly, "I hope you've got a plan."

"I do, Kevin; don't worry. I do," Jerry assures his little brother. "I figured you did, and I have a few ideas myself. It's going to take a lot of work, so I hope you're ready," Jerry asks.

"I am; don't worry," Kevin assured his big brother.

Late that night, after the boys fell asleep...

Their cousin Chuck burst into their bedroom, surprising Kevin and Jerry. Chuck had returned with their mom just in time to help them.

"Hey, guys, look who's here!" Chuck laughed as he jumped on Kevin's bed and then Jerry's. "What?" Kevin groaned, covering his head with a pillow.

"Where's Josh and Vickie?" Jerry asks his younger cousin, thinking to himself how badly they need their help.

"They will be here in a few days. Go back to sleep, boys; we can talk in the morning," Chuck tells the boys to go back to sleep on the couch.

After a night of nightmares, the boys walk to Chuck the next morning, shaking their beds and hollering, "Get up, guys, come on, let's go explore."

"Hold on a minute," Jerry insists, first closing the bedroom door and telling Chuck to sit down. They needed to talk.

"Okay, I know this will sound crazy, but listen." After giving him the rundown the best he knew how, he asks, "Could he help them put an end to the old silver pants?"

With a serious look on Chuck's face, he knew his older cousin wasn't the type to joke or lie when it came to their land. He agrees.

"Just show me what to do because, you know, I got your back. If you get me killed, I will never forgive you."

"Okay, guys," Kevin reminds the boys. "Chores first, let's hurry." So, the boys went to work, rushing through everything to make Mom happy, then to the woods. Making sure they were beyond the tree line, and if anyone came around the house, they couldn't be seen. They began their battle plan. Jerry named it Operation Fairy Swat. First, they gathered small logs and all the vines they could find with everything they already had. The boys got to work sharpening their logs and digging out their traps, following their uncle's instructions for building their giant traps with tinned nets and sharp spikes into the ground and using the vines to pull up. With their swinging traps, the boys weren't taking any chances of the dark fairy making it past the tree line after them. "On the count of three." "1...2...3... Pull, pull." "Now hold," Jerry tells the boys as he ties off the last trap. "Okay, let's go." Jerry steps back, smiling happy with their work.

"Heck yes," Jerry tells the boys. "I'd hate to be that fairy." Chuck tells the boys, "Anyway, where is this evil fairy, guys?" Chuck will soon regret asking the boys.

"Okay, but you have to be quiet. If we take you and show you, Jerry insists on agreeing to take him to their secret spy spot. "Yeah, of course, big brother," Chuck agrees over the hills and through a few more creek beds to the bottom of the bank. Jerry stops and pulls the boys close. "Alright, on the other side of this bank. "Yeah, I remember, because we swing over." Chuck cut him off. "No, Chuck, shh, listen, there is a cave now." Jerry tells him, watching his eyes get big. "What a way!" "Yes." "When we get to the top, don't climb all the way up, or they will see you." "Okay," Jerry tells him.

"Alright, I got you, so the boys climb as quietly as possible, peeking over. "What the crap?" Chuck whispers to Jerry. Sliding back down, I lost for words. After sliding back down, Jerry, with a half-grin, says, "Cat got your tongue?" "Huh." "No, it's just that." "We used to swing, and "Yeah," Kevin spoke up". "We remember."

"Come on, bub!" Jerry quietly laughs at Chuck's response. "Did you think we would do all this work for an imaginary fairy?"

"No, but I wasn't really expecting... Man, she looks like a lady." Wait, no, not the lady. Jerry corrects Chuck, the silver-dressed fairy.

"Wait, there are more creatures"? "Yeah, I told you, the ogre, etc." "Oh yeah, so you were serious about all that?" "Yes, bub," Kevin assures him. Then a fairy ain't all we gotta stop," Chuck asks with a tremble in his voice. Now with a real fear coming over him, wishing he never really asked.

"It's okay, bro, we got this," Jerry says, quietly motioning for them to head home before Mom shouts, giving them away that they are even out there. So, the boys quietly make their way back to the house.

Making their way around the traps, making sure everything was secure, and double-checking everything before they made their way in. Jerry looks at the boys. "We, if you're scared, say you're scared now."

Both boys shook their heads, but really, they were trembling.

"I just hope everything works out, big brother," Chuck says, slapping his older cousin on the shoulder.

"Yeah, me too," Kevin said, slapping his big brother. Jerry pulls on the knotted vines just to make sure they don't slip out before they're cut.

As the boys walk in the back door, they hear their mom yell through.

The house asks, "What was all that banging going on a while ago, boys?" Jerry is quick to answer, "Nothing, Mom. We were building a log cabin." The boys can't help but laugh at him as quietly as possible. Kevin intervenes, "You mean a tree house, MOM?" Well, "whatever you're building, be careful."

"We will," all the boys assure her, and they hurry to the bedroom. After closing the door quietly, Kevin and Jerry go to their beds and lie down. Chuck, who is now coming to terms with the existence of mythical creatures, is now pacing the floor, repeating to himself, "Fairies, ogres, and glowing ladies. I can't believe there are really ogres." "Yeah, bro, ogres," Kevin assures him. Then Jerry lifts his head from the bed and says, "Big giants, scary ogres," and then drops it again.

"Well, we better get some sleep if we're heading out early," Kevin insists. "I am going to work on something. I'll tell you boys what to do in the morning," Jerry tells them, making himself climb up from the bed and now sitting on the side. "You want some help?" Chuck asks him, walking over to his bed.

"We've got to make sure this works," Kevin says, walking over as well. After a few hours of back-and-forth contemplation, the boys all agreed that this plan would work if only they could get old silver pants to chase after them, or at least Chuck.

"Good night, guys. See you in the morning," Chuck tells his cousins, giving them hugs and praying this wasn't their last.

"What are you boys doing?" Mom comes into the room, scaring the daylights out of the boys, unintentionally, with a big smile on her face. "Nothing, Mom; you scared the daylights out of us." Jerry says, giving his mom big hugs and kisses, as well as baby Libby.

Then over to Kevin, and after inspecting their room, Mom gives Kevin the usual gets this and do that, and Kevin gives her the usual Yes, Mom, in the morning, but he never does. Chuck sneaks out in the middle of their discussion.

"Ok" Mom says, "Good night, I love you guys' talk in the morning." "Ok, Mom," the boys agree. Then off to sleep.

Armies of Ogres fighting some army of fairies, seeing the light lady being grabbed and thrown in a cage. Agreeing to something, Jerry can see her nodding but not knowing what. Then he wakes up, covered in sweat. He looks over to see Kevin tossing and turning, "Hey little bro", wake up". He says it's loud enough to wake him. "Stupid ogres, leave them alone", Kevin shouts, raising his voice. "I'm guessing a nightmare", Jerry asks his brother with a half-smile, assuring him, "It's OK, bub". Then off to sleep again, trying to rest before the battle ahead.

Chapter 8
The Fairy Capture Plan

The next morning, the boys wake up to Chucks shaking their beds, then silently setting on Jerry's bed with a scarred look on his face, wondering what their next step was or could possibly be. "Ok, OK, I'm up", Jerry says, not really getting up. Really, because let's get some stuff done so we can, Chuck stops, and with a questioned look, he asks Jerry. "So, I'm the bait"?

"Yes, but not for long, I promise", "Jerry assures him, alright, he agrees to heading out while the boys get ready and lay their camo clothes to the side.

"Dang boys, that was fast" You got the beans hoed out and the corn"? Mom asks, amazed at how quickly the boys finished their chores. After their mom's permission, the boys head out, really not knowing what to expect, but after telling their mom they were playing hide and seek to explain the camo clothes besides Chucks white T, the boys were off to the bank first to see who was out at the cave first. Then, as the boys hoped, there she was: "Ole silver in the now little fairies faces, setting on stumps with fear on their faces, only nodding as ole silver spoke in her for gene language.

The boys slide back down and go over their plan one more time. Remember, bub, Jerry reminds him as soon as "she gets within 5 to 10 feet of the pit; we got her", "me and Kevin will cut the ropes", "OK", Jerry says with as serious a look as possible, knowing this could go horribly in the blink of an eye.

"Alright, make her follow me; get her mad", "I got it" Let's go; you better be ready", Chuck says, watching Kevin go over and climb the tree as Jerry covers himself.

Starting up the back to their peeking spot, Jerry looks up and raises his hand to give Chuck a thumbs up.

And Kevin does as well, from the tree.

Chuck looks over and sees Ole Silver there again, as they planned. Instead of climbing over, Chuck slides back down and starts around, so there is a lot more distance to lead her to her resting place, or so was the plan.

"Hey, fairy," he shouts. She looks up from the little fairy's eyes, saying, "Yeah, your evil demonic creature, come get me!" Chuck shouts, wondering why she's not coming at him.

She speaks in her foreign language, and the little fairies go back into the cave. Kevin hears Chuck shouting and insisting she follow him, so Kevin quickly climbs down, running to Chuck's side. He stands, shouting as well, and they take off running. They look back, and sure enough, here she comes after them.

Jerry, gripping his machete, patiently waits. Sure enough, he feels the boys running right past him, and soon enough, he hears "now."

Jerry jumps to his feet, and with one quick swing of his blade, the boys drop some silver onto the spikes, and through and through she was finished. The boys stare down into the pit, seeing her lifeless body transform into a beautiful white fairy. The boys are just amazed and do not know what to say. Jerry speaks up: "Help me, guys. There is no time to quit. Now help me." So together, the boys brought the log trap back up and tied it off with new vines.

Covering her lifeless body now, Jerry insists they will need her for his next plan to put an end to the ogre as well. The boys go back to the peeping spot and look over there. Sure enough, there was the light lady with a big chain around her neck talking with the little fairies. The boys slide back down, and Jerry raises up, looking at the grays. "Wait, did you guys see how beautiful she is?" "Yes, I did," Chuck replies. "Uh-huh," Kevin replies too.

"Okay, guys, let's get back home. I hope we can get that ogre to follow as well. Without crushing us to death," Chuck is quick to say.

They head back first, making sure the ole silver pants were covered well until morning, and then on to the final, most daring part of their plan, which Jerry prays will work out.

After cleaning up and winding up, the boys floated.

What the plan was and what could happen as a result of the time it took Kevin to climb down and only give them one chance to finish the job, but thank God it worked, and Chuck knew where Jerry was waiting, so he also knew which trap would work while, in the middle of contemplating, the boys hear, 'Hi, Aunt Trish.'

Instantly, they recognized the arrival of their other cousins. After exchanging greetings and hugs with their Aunt Rochell, the children retreated to the bedroom. Jerry briefed Vickie on everything, and although she seemed to think they were a bit crazy, she played along. Jerry, knowing his sister well, said, "I'm serious."

"Yeah, I believe you," Vickie replied, rising from Jerry's bed to give him a playful punch on the arm. "We'll go to see you in the morning, my magical fairy." She hugged him tightly. "I love you, sis. We missed you guys," Jerry reassured her as she headed to the living room. The boys simply shrugged, having nothing else to say. They tidied their beds, turned off the light, and settled in.

As they lay there, Jerry inquired, Chuck, where's your brother?" Chuck, who was sleeping on a bed beside Jerry's, replied, "Oh, I think he went to my dad's. He has a little girl over there." The boys laughed and drifted off to sleep.

Chapter 9

The Ogre's Defeat and a New World

The next morning, as expected, At the top of her lungs, jumping from bed to bed, Vickie exclaims, 'You know, your baby sister is just the most beautiful little baby.' She tells Jerry, trying to take his pillow off his head, laughing and tickling him. 'I know, Vic. Five more minutes, please,' Jerry insists, but then gives up, raising up and thinking of the greater plan and his beautiful little sister.

'Okay, boys,' Vickie tells them, jumping up, and with a loud whisper, she puts her hand to her face and says, 'I want to see your dead fairy,' and with a wink, she shuts the door behind her.

'Okay, guys, let's get it,' Jerry tells the boys, quickly changing his clothes and thinking to himself, should he really get her involved or not? But knowing how they needed her help, he decided to see what Chuck and Kevin thought. 'Alright, boys, it's up to you if we get Vickie involved or not.'

'I don't know,' Chuck says, scratching his head. 'But we could have her on the other side of the biggest trap so the ogre would fall in before it got to her,' Kevin suggests as a plus side to her involvement.

'Yeah, no matter what, we fight together, right?' Jerry says, turning around with fear, almost making him wet his pants as the door rattles.

You guys aren't kidding, huh?" Vickie says, shutting the door quickly with a curious look on her face.

"We told you, sis," Chuck reminds her.

"Ok then, big bro. Let's hear your plan to save this lady and her kids."

"Well, technically," Jerry starts.

"Just spit it out," Vickie tells him, pushing him playfully, trying to lighten the mood.

"Let's go to the woods; it will be easier to explain there." They head out first after saying goodbye to their mom and their aunt. They give their little sister, Miss Liberty, in her purple dress (aunt-brought), hugs and kisses.

"You guys have fun and be careful, ok?" Latricia tells the boys, giving them, all love as well.

"Dang, all this huggy-kissy!" Vickie laughs, pushing the boys out the door and letting her curiosity get the best of her. Through the tree line, Jerry looks around and then back to make sure their moms didn't follow.

"Ok, guys," Jerry says, uncovering Ole Silver, which is now more like a brownish white.

"No, no, no," Vicky says, backing up, still thinking it was all a joke up until this point.

"Guys, you mean to tell me...?"

"Yes, Vic, yes," Kevin interjects. "Everything is true or was true. I didn't lie; none of us did."

"But you can still back out," Chuck replies as well.

"No way. That means there are kids who need us and a lady with a light."

"Yeah, just up around the 'Devil's Backbone,'" Jerry tells her, showing her the traps and going over the plan, demonstrating exactly how they killed the fairy.

"Ok, so let's set her up to be seen, but we can't do this until it's dark."

"Right, that's the plan. Shine this old flashlight on the fairy, and he will run right for her. Then, bam, we cut the vines, and no more Ogre," Kevin assures Vickie.

"Yes, trust us. Once we get over here, we get three tries, but a good hit, and the ogre goes down."

Jerry shows her where to stay while Chuck and Kevin decide where to run to, and they sharpen the stakes in the pit, making sure they're ready.

"Ok, do you need anything? Are we all good?" Jerry checks, and everyone agrees, setting and resting before they head to the cave to spy one last time.

Then, to their surprise, they feel the ground tremble beneath their feet.

"What the heck was that?" Kevin says, looking at his big brother. Then, the most horrible roar, like a lion just yards away, makes them all rush behind a pile of stones and dirt they dug up. Now, to their surprise, the ogre comes to them.

Shaking with fear, machete in hand, all the boys can do is look up at this giant creature. Barely breathing, Jerry could see in the back of his mind that this creature was hurting his baby sister.

Or Mom, or even his little brother, who looked scared to death. So, Jerry watched as the ogre backed up, turning around and sniffing the air as if it could smell the fairy.

"One more step," Jerry said to himself, and to his surprise, one more step it was. The big dummy leaned over their trap, not knowing he was leaning in the line of fire. Jerry and Kevin, with the same thing in mind, cut both vines, releasing the logs, and smacked both logs, making an impact, one to the head and one to the backside, sending it to its death into the pit where it will remain forever.

"Wow, did that just happen?" Vickie shouts, jumping up and chuckling, and the boys now run over, grab sticks, and shove them down to make sure the job was done.

"Guys, help me," Jerry tells them, grasping one side of the fairy; they grab the other and toss her in as well. "Ok, before we cover them up," "It's getting too cold, guys," Vickie tells them, with a half-grin and her arms crossed. Jerry gives her his jacket and says, "This can wait; let's check on the kids." Around the corner, they see such a bright white light that they have to squint their eyes.

"I see you over there," they hear from a distance. "Uh, yeah, are you okay?" said Miss Lady. "Yes, Jerry, I'm fine now, thanks to you all."

As their eyes adjusted, the guys couldn't believe their eyes. Really, neither could Vickie.

"Where did the kids go?" Jerry asks her. "Home," she is quick to answer, "as soon as my power was restored at the death of the ugly obra in which you brave young men bravely done."

"Yeah, we did," Kevin says with a big smile.

Jerry looks at her and can't help but ask, "An Obra." "Yes, it's a horrible ugly," "I guess Ogre," you would call it in your world", but the real name is an evil Obra. "He held me captive after many years, making me use my power for evil. This cave was to create more evil fairies to also do their will." Dang, this is all too real, Vickie says, shaking her head and looking at the chains lying on the stone.

"So how did you get out of these things," she asks, clanging them together. They were Obra-enchanted chains, and you are very lucky, guys, and gals that you are so smart. "Well, what now, moss light lady," Kevin asks, starting to get chilly as well.

"Well, I truly want you all to know that in my world, you would all be great heroes, and how would we get there?" Chuck asks, looking into the cave. "Yes, Chuck, through there." "But first, I must go set things right." "Huh, what do you mean?" Jerry asks.

Yes, through the cave, but there are a few more Obra's through there. I will handle myself. They are waiting for more kids to come through, but just know the cave is here, and I will return soon to not only reward you but to show you my world if you want to see it.

"Yes, yes, they all agree." "After you get rid of the Obra's, that is from there." I assure you; my heroes are coming soon. "Also, the cave will remain. It is my creation," That is, if it's okay with you guys." "Yeah, it's fine," Jerry says. "As long as no more fairies or Obra's come through."

"Agreed," now I must go set my sisters free to rid our world of the Obra stench in my world." "By the way my name is Arabella, here she's reaching out her hand with four stones she hands to the kids.

"What are these"? Vickie asks, picking one up, thinking how beautiful they were. "You can keep them or do what you wish. I've kept them hidden from the Obra for many years until we finally found this world. You brave young men, set me free, and lady." She says she is smiling and waving as she steps into the cave.

Then, with a bright white flash, they were all standing in the boys' room, holding their stones.

The door swings open, Mom looks in. "I didn't hear you guys come in." "Oh, yeah, a while ago," Jerry assures her, sitting on his bed. Then Vickie, and Chuck goes over to his blanket on the floor and sits down, all of them lost for words.

Chapter 10
The Mysterious Stones and Vanishing Cave

Early in the next morning, Jerry wakes up to Kevin shaking his bed and saying, "Come on, bub, get up, let's go." He wanted them to go check if Arabella had returned or if the cave was still there.

They all got dressed and headed out through the tree line, past their traps, and up to the devil's backbone.

And just as the boys and Hady expected, the cave was still there, sort of.

"What the hell? Did you guys see that?" Jerry asked, raising up from their spying position. "Okay, right when things couldn't get any worse," Vickie said, wanting to get closer but afraid. From inside the cave, they could see flashes of different colored lights: blue, then white, and even red at one point.

"Guys, I'm freaking out," Kevin said, scratching his head, and all of a sudden, nothing happened. Yes, literally, the cave and all vanished.

The kids quickly stepped over the hill to investigate, and everything was the way it once was—not even the tracks from the creature were there.

"Wait, this can't be," Jerry said, picking up a branch and showing the others where the tracks should have been. "We know," Chuck reminded everyone. "She said the cave would always be there." "Yeah, I heard her too," Vickie agreed.

"Anyway," Kevin started to say before he was cut short by his mom yelling for them.

The kids rushed back as fast as possible to their mom with a mad face standing on the porch.

"Where did you guys get this stone?" She asked, holding it for them to see.

"We found it, honestly, Mom," Jerry told her. "Well, I found out a few things about it." "What, Mom?" Kevin asked, all the kids staring with puzzled looks on their faces. "Hold on," the boys' aunt said. "Can you find any more?" "Well, I got one," Vickie told her mom. "Yeah, me too," Chuck said, also reaching over to their mom. "Yeah, we each got one," Kevin said, giving his over.

"Well, if you run across any, bring them to us," Trish told them. "My friend, who's a gemologist, says they're not of this planet. So, boys, there are going to be some changes around here, and your dads on his way home." She grabbed her kids, hugged them tight, and kissed their heads.

"Where's Rick?" their aunt shouted, then apologized. "I am sorry, but guys, the one stone. He told us we could name it what we wanted because it shouldn't exist." "Yes, guys," so I'm looking up the others, and we can't tell anyone about these, okay." They all agreed and decided to celebrate. But in the back of their minds, all they could think of was the cave and the light lady.

"It's the more difficult roads that lead to the most beautiful destinations."